Original title:
The House We Make Together

Copyright © 2025 Creative Arts Management OÜ
All rights reserved.

Author: Atticus Thornton
ISBN HARDBACK: 978-1-80587-078-4
ISBN PAPERBACK: 978-1-80587-548-2

Embracing the Everyday

In socks that never match, we stride,
With breakfast crumbs we take in pride.
The dog steals more than just a shoe,
While I debate if pants are due.

The plants all cheer, or so I think,
As I forget to give a drink.
Their leaves droop low, in silent jest,
Yet still they thrive, they are the best.

The fridge hums songs of takeout nights,
While laundry piles give me frights.
Yet in this chaos, laughter blooms,
As socks and spoons fill empty rooms.

We juggle lives like circus clowns,
With half-baked dreams and silly frowns.
As love and laughter take the stage,
Together, we write our own page.

Bridges of Trust

We built a bridge with silly jokes,
Hoping it wouldn't fall with pokes.
Each laugh a plank, each grin a beam,
Wobbling like a wacky dream.

Our trust is glue, it has no doubt,
Even if we laugh too loud.
Through all the quirks, we find our way,
Swaying like it's a dance parade.

Shared Shadows Under One Sky

In shadows long, we chase the light,
Twirling 'round like kids at night.
The moon a lamp for our silly dance,
Under its glow, we take a chance.

Falling sideways, laughs cascade,
The stars join in, a twinkling parade.
Each mishap brings a giggly shout,
In our shared shadows, joy's about.

Song of Our Sanctuary

In our nook, where giggles hum,
Laughter's rhythm, a beating drum.
We sing loud tunes of silly cheer,
Inviting all to join right here.

Off-key notes, we gleefully shout,
Echoes bouncing 'round, no doubt.
Inside our walls, jokes bounce around,
Creating harmony, joy unbound.

Crafted Connections

We stitch our tales with thread of fun,
Even if it comes undone.
Every story, a patch we sew,
In this quilt, our colors glow.

Through mismatched squares, we find a way,
Each snag a laugh, brightening the day.
With every stitch, our bond is strong,
In crafting joy, we all belong.

Dreams Woven in Wood

In a wooden box we play,
With crayons drawn, we slay.
A castle made from squeaky shoes,
Where pink elephants sip on brews.

Giraffes dance in the living room,
While the cats plot their grand zoom.
Walls echo giggles and chirps,
As the dog performs wiggly burps.

Hearth of Hearts

Our hearth's a cozy grill,
For laughter, spice, and silly thrill.
We roast up dreams, no need for s'mores,
As next-door penguins knock on doors.

With marshmallow clouds passing by,
We toast to pizza in the sky.
Our hearts sing louder than the choir,
As jellybeans dance on a wire.

Union of Walls

Our walls are stacked with giggles high,
Made of marshmallows, oh my, oh my!
With duct tape dreams and a twist of fate,
We'll throw a party till it's late.

The floor is lava, don't you dare,
Jump from the couch, but beware!
The windows wink, the doors do sway,
In this lively place, we laugh and play.

Together We Build

We build with laughter, bricks of fun,
Each room aglow with cheer, we run.
A sprinkle of magic in every seam,
Our wildest thoughts align, it seems.

The roof is made of jelly beans,
Our dreams flow in like sunny streams.
A dance floor where the kittens shake,
As we create our grandly make.

Roots and Resonance

In the garden, weeds do dance,
Claiming space while we take a chance.
Roots entwine, a tangled jest,
Nature laughing at our quest.

Branches sway, a wobbly show,
Who knew plants could steal the flow?
As we nurture, each leaf's a prank,
Roots giggle, 'Thanks for the bank!'

Threads of Togetherness

Sewing dreams in quirky patterns,
Threads of laughter, friendship flattens.
Spools of joy, a stitching spree,
Making memories, you and me.

Needles dart, stories blend,
Creating chaos, what a trend!
With every stitch the fabric sways,
A patchwork of our funny days.

Interwoven Lives

Like tangled headphones in my bag,
Our lives entwined, never a drag.
You pull a thread, I tug it too,
What a mess, but feels brand new!

A jigsaw puzzle missing pieces,
But laughter grows as tension ceases.
Together we make quite the scene,
Interwoven, but still serene.

The Pulse of Shared Spaces

In this room, a dance we'd dare,
High-fives echo, flying hair!
Coffee spills, oh what a sight,
Laughter bounces, feeling bright.

The fridge hums a disco tune,
Out of tune, but none too soon.
We pulse together, loud and clear,
A symphony of joy and cheer.

Shared Spaces

In the kitchen, there's always a clash,
With spatulas flying, and pots that crash.
We dance between crumbs, we jive with pride,
As flour coats the floor like a big white tide.

The living room's chaos, a sock on the lamp,
A cat in a bag, what a curious champ!
We trip on each other, laugh 'til we cry,
As snacks in the couch cushions silently lie.

Roofs of Resilience

Under this roof, the weather's a joke,
With leaky old pipes that constantly poke.
We gather and giggle, each drip a refrain,
While dodging the drops like it's all a game.

Time to repair, but who has the skill?
With duct tape and dreams, we handle the thrill.
We build with our laughter, our hearts in a knot,
This patchwork of life—oh, it means quite a lot!

Where Laughter Lingers

In every corner, a story awaits,
Of socks on the ceiling, and playful debates.
We dive into memories, we dig up the fun,
As each cranny sparkles with laughter well-spun.

The hallway's a gallery, framed smiles everywhere,
With goofy expressions that hang in the air.
A tribute to moments, absurd, yet so true,
Where giggles abide, and frowns bid adieu.

Safe Haven

Here in this shelter, the wildness runs free,
With pranks in the pantry, and glee by the tree.
A wacky concoction of life, love, and play,
We juggle our chaos, come what may.

When the world seems too heavy, we lighten the load,
Swapping tales and chuckles, we stroll down the road.
With open hearts and a swing in our stride,
This cozy corner's where joy will reside.

Hearth of Hearts

In a kitchen where chaos thrives,
Spaghetti's flying, oh how it dives!
We dance through the flour, twirling with glee,
Who knew pasta could set our spirits free?

The fire crackles, a warmth so grand,
S'mores stick to fingers, we make quite a stand.
With stories that bubble and laughter that flows,
Our love sits around like marshmallows in rows.

Weaving Memories

In the living room, we play charades,
Wild gestures and faces, the best masquerades!
A dog in pajamas steals the show,
He's the cast star, don't you know?

Pillows become forts, where dreams come alive,
A kingdom of giggles, where all can thrive.
With legends of bobbles and spills we narrate,
Each tale is a treasure that we celebrate.

Rooms Filled with Laughter

The bathroom's a splashing, bubbly old mess,
Rubber ducks float in their royal dress.
We sing in the shower, a concert so loud,
Even the neighbors cheer and feel proud!

The bedroom's a site for pillow fight wars,
Feathered explosions, we're laughter's young scores.
As we tussle and tumble, the clock ticks away,
In the chaos of fun, we all want to stay.

Unity in Every Corner

In hallways adorned with photos of smiles,
Nostalgic tales travel for miles.
With socks on the floor and shoes at the door,
We stylishly trip, but still ask for more.

The garage holds secrets of dreams yet to bloom,
A disco ball shines in the tool-filled room.
With every misstep and clumsy delight,
Together we shine, even through the night.

A Haven of Hope

In a space where socks go to hide,
We search for the missing shoes with pride.
Pajamas on chairs, a cozy scene,
Beneath the mess, love reigns supreme.

We argue over snacks, and who took the last,
Yet laughter echoes, the good times amassed.
With every spilled drink, and pillow fight,
Our little chaos ignites pure delight.

The Symphony We Create

It's a dance of mismatched plates on the floor,
A concert of clinks when we open the door.
Harmony found in the clatter and cheer,
As we brew coffee, our laughter's sincere.

Off-key serenades from the shower's small space,
Making music together, at our own silly pace.
Tangled in rhythm, we stumble and sway,
Creating our symphony, day after day.

Brick by Brick

With every new project, we argue a lot,
Who dropped the paint? Oh, how I forgot!
Yet from the debris, creativity flows,
Building a fortress where hilarity grows.

Each brick is a story, a laugh, and a sigh,
A fortress of jest, reaching up to the sky.
Through mishaps and hiccups, we fashion a place,
Where joy is the glue, and love's the embrace.

Under One Roof

In a snug little haven where odd socks reside,
We trip over toys, and yet we won't hide.
The floors dance with crumbs from our last meal,
But the laughter we share is what gives it appeal.

The walls may be crooked, the fridge slightly stinks,
But together we find joy in the smallest of kinks.
With mismatched furniture and giggles so loud,
Under one roof, we make each other proud.

Walls That Hold Whispered Secrets

In the quiet of night, secrets take flight,
Socks in the dryer, oh what a sight!
The cat's on the ceiling, the dog's in a craze,
Baffled by whispers, we all get amazed.

Painted with laughter, each wall has its tale,
A shoe that went missing, we'll follow the trail.
With echoes of giggles, we fill every space,
In this baffling castle, we find our own place.

Embracing Every Corner

In a nook full of books, a tiny gnome grins,
He hides with the dust bunnies, plotting our sins.
The kitchen's a playground, where spoons like to dance,
And the fridge hums a tune, just to enhance.

The bathroom's a jungle, the mirror can chat,
With toothpaste adventures, oh, where's my hat?
Each corner, a treasure, a laughter-filled nook,
In this wild maze of living, come take a look!

Colors of Togetherness

We splatter the walls with weird, vibrant hues,
Like a rainbow gone crazy, who wore those shoes?
A canvas of chaos, we splash and we play,
In this artistic mess, we find joy every day.

With mismatched cushions and curtains askew,
We lounge like royalty, oh, who needs a view?
The scribbles of children, the art of delight,
Each color a memory, our lives burst with light.

Harmony in Foundation

Beneath our strange roof, the floorboards all creak,
They dance to the rhythm of fun, so unique.
As we trip on our dreams, with glee, we all shout,
'This foundation of laughter is what it's about!'

In the corners we sing, our voices collide,
While the neighbors just wonder what's cooking inside.
From the roof to the roots, our heartbeats align,
In this quirky abode, together we shine.

Whispering Echoes

In the corner, socks do dance,
They pair up in a wild romance.
The cat stares, plotting its scheme,
While we're lost in a silly dream.

Loud laughter echoes, fills the air,
Chasing dust bunnies, everywhere.
The plants gossip, they sway and tease,
While we sip tea, and share our pleas.

A fridge hums tunes of ancient lore,
As leftovers break into a roar.
Each creak of floorboards tells a tale,
Of mishaps that make mundane things pale.

In this realm of whimsy and light,
Every moment feels just right.
Wacky as it, together we'll stay,
In the sweet chaos of our day.

Foundation of Us

We built a life on mismatched chairs,
With cushions claiming heartfelt cares.
We've bargains struck in playful spats,
And banter that could knock off hats.

Our pantry's filled with odd delights,
Like pickles dressed in funny tights.
Each meal's an adventure, take a chance,
On flavors that give our tongues a dance.

We paint the walls with colors bright,
A canvas of our joyous flight.
The plumbing's sometimes quite a mess,
Yet laughter hides our soft distress.

Through each quirk, and little surprise,
We see the world through love-filled eyes.
In every corner, joy's a plus,
In the foundation that's really us.

Love Anchored in Stone

Our hearts are tied with silly string,
With every faux pas, they still cling.
A mountain of laundry, high and wide,
Yet together, we enjoy the ride.

We share our fears, our hopes, our dreams,
In whispered jokes and silly schemes.
Every bumpy path we have walked,
With laughter shared, it's love we've locked.

The echoes of our joyful fights,
Light up the house on starry nights.
Through all the stacked-up socks and kin,
The chaos wraps us safely in.

So here's to our quirky, strange abode,
Where every love note is a code.
In this shelter where laughter is grown,
Our love stands steady, like anchored stone.

Sheltered Souls

Two quirky souls in one big space,
Chasing each other in a race.
The dog is barking at the moon,
While we hum along a silly tune.

We built a fort with blankets long,
Inside it, we found where we belong.
A fortress, slight, yet oh so grand,
Made from giggles and a rubber band.

The coffee pot sings our morning song,
In harmony, we can't go wrong.
We search for spoons in the oddest places,
Finding fun in our shared embraces.

Through cluttered rooms and joyful sighs,
The laughter bubbles and never dies.
In each other's arms, we've truly found,
A home where even silliness is profound.

A Home in Harmony

In our cozy space, where socks go missing,
A treasure hunt begins, oh what a blessing.
We trip on toys, and laugh out loud,
A joyful chorus, a playful crowd.

Cups stacked high, a leaning tower,
Coffee spills, but we never cower.
The waiter's role is always mine,
As I juggle snacks and craft our dine.

At dinner time, it's a wild ride,
Who eats whose food? We won't abide!
With funny faces and jokes galore,
Our laughter echoes through every door.

So here's our tale, in quirky tune,
Where every day feels like a cartoon.
A laughter-filled life, let it persist,
In this wacky space, we surely exist.

Walls of Affection

These walls hold secrets, a zoo of quirks,
Where silly dances and laughter lurks.
A cat parade across the dining chair,
With giggles shared, it's beyond compare.

Our fridge is a canvas, magnets all around,
Masterpieces made, where joy is found.
The dog's stuffed toys, scattered with flair,
He plays hide and seek, without a care.

In this patchwork space, chaos is king,
We share odd moments that make us sing.
With sticky notes, reminders of fun,
Our silly saga has only begun.

Each crack in the wall holds a tale of cheer,
Of vines and stains that we hold dear.
We love our mess, our joyful mess,
In this quirky realm, we truly bless.

Crafted with Care

In this quirky nook, we craft with flair,
With mismatched chairs and a tattered chair.
Doodle-filled notebooks, ideas abound,
While cats plot mischief, we're homeward bound.

A cupboard of snacks, a brave delight,
Countless adventures, all day and night.
Juggling chores, yet we share a laugh,
Building memories is our secret craft.

Sticky fingers paint the kitchen bright,
With laughter and flour, oh what a sight!
Our bonds get stronger with every spill,
In this space of wonders, we find our thrill.

So here's to our refuge, full of glee,
With ticklish moments and fun, you'll see.
In a world of chaos, we're quite the pair,
Crafted with love, beyond compare.

Gathered Moments

Gathered 'round the couch, leg wrestling spree,
With giggles and pokes, what fun it'll be!
Snacks in hand, we strategize the game,
With victory dances, we're all to blame.

The dog steals a slipper, it's a heist, you see,
His eyes full of mischief, as happy as can be.
Each day in our joint, a playful affair,
With laughter that dances, drifting in the air.

When friends come to visit, it's a joyous mess,
Board games galore, no time to stress.
Somehow we spill drinks like a wild dream,
But in our shenanigans, laughter's the theme.

So here's to the moments, the giggles, the fun,
In our joyful chaos, we're never done.
With every shared laugh, our hearts grow wide,
In this zany whirlwind, we always abide.

Sunlight Through Our Windows

Sunlight spills over breakfast plates,
Pancakes in stacks, impossible fates.
Syrup rivers flow, sweet and wide,
While shadows dance on the playful side.

Coffee cups argue about who's best,
Whispers of laughter, never a jest.
The walls are filled with silly shout,
Echoes of joy that we can't live without.

The Heartbeat of Home

Our fridge hums tunes no one can hear,
Its secrets held close, never too near.
Leftovers on shelves doing a jig,
While takeout boxes all wear a wig.

Neighbors peek in, curious stares,
They think we've a circus with lions and bears.
But it's just us cats with tails all aflight,
Creating a show every single night.

Spaces Between Us

The couch is a ship in a sea of socks,
Where battles of laundry are won with a box.
Remote control fights, the latest craze,
Navigating channels in a comedic maze.

Hiding behind pillows, there's giggling galore,
As we forage for snacks from the disheveled floor.
Each cushion a fortress, each laugh a delight,
Adventures abound until the starlight.

Paintings of Our Past

Frames hold memories, crooked and quirky,
The art of our lives, slightly murky.
Grandma's vase and a doodle or two,
Each piece has a story, some funny, some blue.

Every knock on the door, laughter's the key,
Welcoming guests like old friends, you see.
In this gallery of chaos, we all take part,
Each moment a brush stroke, each laugh a fine art.

Love's Light Through Windows

In a place where laughter roams,
We dance like shadows in the gloams.
Coffee spills on the kitchen floor,
While we giggle and beg for more.

Sock puppets tell our secret tales,
As we plot to take down the snails.
Chasing dust bunnies, what a sight,
Each corner holds our shared delight.

We've got a map of silly dreams,
Drawn in crayon and goofy themes.
When the cat steals the cozy chair,
We argue who's next for freedom's air.

Through brightened panes, the sun peeks in,
Promising mischief with a grin.
In this space where joy is free,
Every light makes a memory.

Souls Intertwined

With a grin, a twinkle in the eye,
We spin our stories, oh so spry.
Jumping jacks in the living room,
Who knew that joy could burst and bloom?

Mismatched socks tell our wild tales,
As laughter and pizza fill the scales.
Our hearts are like a pizza pie,
Topped with dreams that soar and fly.

Under the table, whispers gleam,
Branches of our silly, shared dream.
The world gets blurry, and we laugh,
Silly moments, our photograph.

With every hug, we intertwine,
Creating madness, oh so fine.
In this tangled space we stay,
Chasing clouds that race away.

Gathered Under One Light

We gather 'round in mismatched chairs,
With laughter tangled in our hairs.
A shadow puppet show unfolds,
Where every monster's story's told.

Rainbows painted on the walls,
As we take turns and spin like balls.
Tacos and laughter fill our nights,
While silly songs take playful flights.

Under one shining ceiling bright,
Cuddling close through the thick of night.
With ice cream droops and silly fights,
Creating our own joy-filled heights.

Every glance, a sparkling cue,
Our bond's a riddle, tried and true.
It's magic in the everyday,
As we laugh our little cares away.

Foundation of Memories

In this quirky little zone,
Every tile tells tales of our own.
A trampoline for our endless shots,
Each kind of chaos, love's sweet knots.

With a pun that sticks like glue,
We build our dreams with a wink or two.
From cereal spills to fuzzy socks,
We chuckle at time's sudden knocks.

Each closet hides our secrets bold,
Wrapped in laughter, never cold.
From broken toys to silly fights,
Our stories dance in the moonlight.

Memories piled, like books on shelves,
In our hearts, we gather ourselves.
So here's the plan: let's never part,
For this laughter is a work of art.

Secrets Beneath the Roof

In the attic, dusty and bright,
We found a squirrel took flight.
His acorns hidden with great care,
We laughed as he gave us a stare.

The basement holds a mystery,
Who painted walls with such history?
A spaghetti monster, we now know,
Plays hide and seek beneath the glow.

A cat that thinks he's king, you see,
Turns our dining chairs to royalty.
He rules with a fuzzy little paw,
While we simply sit in awe.

In corners, old shoes gather dust,
Each pair holds a journey, we trust.
We share their stories with a grin,
As we toss them out, the laughter spins.

Tapestry of Togetherness

We tried to bake a pie one day,
Flour flew in a silly spray.
Sugar landed on the cat,
Now he's sweet, imagine that!

The living room turned to a stage,
Impromptu plays, we set the gauge.
With socks for puppets, laughter roared,
An Oscar nod we all adored.

At dinner time, our table's packed,
Who knew there's art in food that's racked?
A mountain of mashed, like Everest,
We ate and laughed, oh what a quest!

Dancing dust bunnies held the floor,
As we twirled till we could no more.
Our living room, a dance site grand,
With moves that only we could stand.

Echoes of Affection

Morning coffee spills with a sigh,
A dog chases shadows, oh my!
His bark jingles like wind chimes dear,
As we sip our brew, full of cheer.

In the hallway, secrets do creep,
Whispers of stories that never sleep.
We giggle softly as we share,
Who draped the toilet with a flair?

Our game nights often get absurd,
When the charades turn to a word.
Hints get mixed, from pop to pop,
We end with laughter, can't stop!

At night, we play hide-and-seek,
But it's the cat that we can't pique.
For he sleeps while we search all round,
Only to find him snoring sound.

The Nest We Nurture

We crafted beds of pillows high,
A fort so grand it touched the sky.
Yet one light sneeze brought it down,
"Is that your fault?" asks the frown.

Crafting messes is our true art,
With crayons, paints, we make a start.
But walls are now a canvas of fun,
With every stroke, our laughter's spun.

Our garden grew, but not alone,
A raccoon made it his throne.
He steals the veggies, oh what a thief,
Yet we'll count his antics as our relief.

Each weekend brings a new surprise,
From board games to glittery skies.
In every corner, joy's parade,
A nest of love, that we've all made.

A Canvas of Commitment

We paint our walls with laughter's hue,
Each messy splotch tells tales anew.
With mismatched furniture and crooked frames,
We smile and giggle, forgetting our names.

The dog is barking, the cat's on the ledge,
The plants are dubious, we gave them a pledge.
With cooking disasters and burnt toast so grand,
We wave our forks like a silly band.

Under the disco ball, we dance and twirl,
In our kingdom of chaos, let joy unfurl!
With socks on our heads, we declare it's a day,
Of pillow fights and treasure hunts on display.

We'll paint our dreams, both big and small,
With a splash of whimsy, we'll conquer it all.
Together we'll craft this wild, crazy spree,
Our canvas of commitment, just you and me.

Seeds of Togetherness

We planted hope in a pot so small,
With seeds of laughter, we watch them sprawl.
The carrots are wiggly, the radishes grin,
As we water with giggles, the fun can begin!

In the garden of mishaps, we grow our pride,
With weeds full of charm, we won't let them hide.
Strange vegetables dance in our crazy plot,
We'll feast on our harvest, if edible, why not?

We share the mess from our mud-caked shoes,
And sing silly songs about garden blues.
With watering cans spilling our newest thyme,
Together we flourish, one joyful rhyme.

As sunflowers wink in the bright, warm light,
We hoot and we holler, our hearts take flight.
In this fertile chaos, our love will sprout,
With roots intertwined, leaving no room for doubt.

Beyond the Threshold

With open doors that squeak and sway,
We welcome the nonsense that comes our way.
The welcome mat's frayed, but it holds our cheer,
As we stumble in giggles, no worries here!

Our quirky decor tells stories untold,
From rubber ducks in the bathroom to treasures of old.
With mismatched socks that dance on the floor,
We embrace the delightful, there's always more!

We greet the mailman with silly affairs,
Offering cake with sprinkles, no time for stares.
We'll paint the town with our quirky finesse,
Beyond the threshold, zero stress!

So come on in, pass the chaos around,
In our loud little world, fun is the sound.
With open hearts and smiles that gleam,
We'll make every moment a wacky dream.

Light That Binds

In our electrifying living room glow,
The light above flickers, puts on a show.
With shadow puppets dancing on the wall,
We giggle and ponder, do they know it all?

The flash of our smiles, the warmth in our hearts,
With each silly jest, a new moment starts.
The kitchen light flickers, as if it's alive,
And we charm it with laughter, our spirits thrive.

From movie marathons to popcorn fights,
Our laughter ignites—what a wondrous sight!
With friends all around, and stories to tell,
We bask in the glow, all is quite swell.

So let's keep it bright, let humor entwine,
In this magical space, where we dine and align.
With the light that binds us, we'll always find cheer,
In shadows or bright, it's love that we steer.

Together We Anchor

In a boat made of laughter, we float,
Sailing the sea with a quirky goat.
Our anchor's a rubber, just watch it bounce,
We'll drift off to places that make us pounce.

Jellyfish dance while we sing a tune,
Our capes are made from a giant balloon.
We've tossed all convention to the wind,
And in this silly ride, we'll never rescind.

With friends in our pockets, we twist and twirl,
Even the waves join our wacky whirl.
A treasure map scribbled on a pizza pie,
Captains of chaos, just my friends and I.

We'll anchor at dusk, with stars as our guide,
Sharing tall tales, with giggles inside.
Together we chuckle through wild, windy groans,
Creating a world that feels like our own.

Simmering in Sunlight

Under a sky that's a coconut hue,
We dance on the lawn in mismatched shoe.
Sunlight is sizzling like bacon on toast,
We barbecue dreams, oh, let's celebrate most!

With lemonade rivers we splash and we play,
Our shadows are laughing, come join the ballet.
Ice cream is melting, we're tossing it high,
A treat turns to giggles, oh my, oh my!

Laughter's our spice, a dash of delight,
As we twirl like dancers beneath the bright light.
Whimsical whispers float through the air,
We're simmering dreams, without a care.

As sunshine dips low and colors ignite,
We cherish this moment, our joy takes flight.
In a bowl full of smiles, we feast all day,
Together we cook up our own fun buffet.

Sanctuary of Souls

In a quirky old barn, where shadows are friends,
We gather our stories and mix the trends.
With each silly dance, the hay starts to bounce,
Our sanctuary shimmies, we twirl and pounce.

Old quilts and giggles pile up on the floor,
Where whisks are mighty and spatulas roar.
We bake up our dreams with a pinch of cheer,
And serve laughter soup for everyone here.

Candles are winking, our shadows strike poses,
We tickle the moments that life often throws us.
Each giggle a fortress, as warm as the sun,
In our playful castle, we're never done.

With joy as our compass, we navigate through,
This haven of nonsense, where hearts feel anew.
In a sanctuary vibrant, with love all around,
Together we blossom, in laughter we're found.

Affectionate Arches

Beneath arches of smiles, we march hand in hand,
Building a world that is funny and grand.
With silly umbrellas and hats made of cheese,
We paint our adventures, oh please, oh please.

Jumping on trampolines strung up in the air,
We sway with the breeze, not a worry or care.
As giggles fly high, we dive into dreams,
Creating a canvas of bright, wiggly beams.

With twinkling lights dancing above our heads,
We craft our own magic, dodging all dreads.
A parade of balloons, we float and we spin,
With each goofy flip, we're ready to win.

Two arching rainbows lead on to the fun,
We laugh 'til we glow, two friends become one.
In this crafted realm of affection and play,
We cherish each moment, come what may.

Rooms Filled with Grace

In the kitchen, where chaos reigns,
We dance with spatulas, ignore the stains.
Burnt toast is a badge of our delight,
We laugh through breakfast, morning's bright.

The living room's a jungle, what a sight,
With cushions flying, oh what a fright!
We trip on shoes, a pile so grand,
Together we giggle, it's just as planned.

Our bedrooms echo with whispers and dreams,
Fort-building magic and silly schemes.
The cat judges us from his lofty throne,
In a kingdom of laughter, we're never alone.

In hallways adorned with sticky notes,
We've written our rules, and shared our quotes.
Every corner holds tales of our days,
Reverse-gravity moments in so many ways.

The Spirit of Togetherness

In the garden, shovels in hand,
We dig for treasure, or so we planned.
We argue on what flower should bloom,
While plants conspire to take up more room.

The bathroom's a circus, toothpaste galore,
We slip on the floor, then laugh some more.
Hairbrush in hand, we sing out of tune,
Our very own concert, just past noon.

Dining room debates on pizza or stew,
With toppings galore, it's hard to choose!
We feast on laughter as crumbs take flight,
Tablecloth battles are quite a sight.

And when the sun sets, we gather 'round,
With stories of bravery and laughter loud.
In the glow of friendship, we can't help but cheer,
Together we thrive, year after year.

Nestled Dreams

Under blankets, we hide from the world,
In pillow fort castles, our laughter unfurled.
Monsters are silly, their roars just a joke,
With giggles and shadows, our courage awoke.

In the playroom, where chaos is king,
We ride on our bikes, and pretend we're in spring.
The floor is lava, oh no, what to do?
Leap to the couch, I'll rescue you too!

Outside we race, with kites in the air,
The wind tries to snag them, but we just don't care.
We tumble and tumble, till giggles do cease,
With scraped-up knees, we find our release.

As bedtime rolls in and dreams softly climb,
Our whispers drift off, in rhythm and rhyme.
Nestled in laughter, we drift into sleep,
In small moments shared, our memories keep.

Foundations of Friendship

With a toolbox of whimsy, we build up our glee,
Crafting conversations, just you and me.
Screws and giggles, a hammer of fun,
Constructing our stories 'til day is done.

In the backyard, we pit our games right,
A slip and slide river, oh what a sight!
We laugh through the splashes, our battles are grand,
In the sun's warm embrace, we take a stand.

Around the fire, we share tales galore,
Of epic adventures and mythical lore.
We roast marshmallows for sweet little treats,
With sticky fingers, we can't be beat!

Each room has a heartbeat, a rhythm unique,
We weave in the moments, it's laughter we seek.
In this quirky abode, our hearts intertwine,
In the fabric of friendship, forever we shine.

Tapestry of Togetherness

In our abode of quirky flair,
Laughter bounces off the chair.
A cat that thinks it runs the show,
And dogs who dance like pros, you know.

Pizza nights with toppings wild,
Even the broccoli, it's so reviled!
We trip on toys and laugh aloud,
In this madhouse, we feel proud.

The fridge adorned with art so bright,
Crayon scribbles, a delightful sight.
Every room a tale to tell,
Of sock fights and ice cream spells.

Though chaos reigns in every space,
Each mess reflects our goofy grace.
In our hearts, we can't complain,
Embracing joy, we'll share the strain.

Memories Beneath the Beams

Under beams where secrets hide,
We sneak in snacks, oh what a ride!
In the attic, treasures we find,
Old board games, laughter intertwined.

A couch that squeaks with every flop,
Our dance moves make the neighbors stop.
Spaghetti fights on a Tuesday night,
Who knew food could take to flight?

We hoard the silly and the sweet,
With mismatched socks on our dancing feet.
The walls have heard our loudest dreams,
And all our laughter, like playful streams.

Beneath these beams, our stories blend,
In each goofy moment, we transcend.
A family tapestry, woven tight,
In memories, we find our light.

Embracing Shelter

In this shelter built from cheer,
Every giggle, we hold dear.
A roof that bends to our odd ways,
Comfy chaos fills our days.

Juggling chores in wild parade,
We trip on life, but never fade.
Pillow fights and ice cream spills,
A home of laughter always thrills.

The garden's wild with toys and greens,
A jungle gym befitting queens.
We dance with dust bunnies on the floor,
As giggles echo, we ask for more.

Under this quirky, loving dome,
We bask in bliss, we've found our home.
The heartbeats blend in funny tunes,
As we create our wacky boons.

Unity in Every Room

In every room, a quirky sight,
From messy art to breakfast bites.
Sibling squabbles and silly fights,
Yet love beams bright like city lights.

In the kitchen, things go boom,
As flour clouds fill the room.
A recipe gone astray,
Turns into giggles, brightening the day.

Each corner holds a playful grin,
With goofy antics, we dive in.
The laundry's piled high like peaks,
Yet in the mess, our laughter speaks.

Our home's a stage for silly flair,
In unity, we dance and share.
Through every laugh, every room,
Love blooms bright, dispelling gloom.

Guiding Lights

We gather all our socks in a pile,
Try to match them up with a smile,
Yet all we find are lonely pairs,
They're having a party, who even cares?

The kitchen's a blend of spices and mess,
With three cooks, it's a culinary stress,
We stir the pot and some small fights,
But laughter erupts like the late-night bites.

The bathroom's a race for the last drop of soap,
We barter and trade, trying to cope,
With toothpaste wars and towel dilemmas,
In this circus show, we're all the comedians.

With our quirky ways and playful blunders,
The bond we share is a joy that thunders,
Through mishaps and giggles, we take flight,
In the chaos of living, everything feels right.

Unity Above

In a world where chaos sometimes reigns,
We make our plans with silly campaigns,
With charts and graphs to organize brunch,
But who'll clean the dishes? Well, that's up for punch.

The living room filled with cushions galore,
It's a fortress, a landscape, a junkyard floor,
We dive in with laughter, all in the game,
Finding lost treasures—who's to blame?

Battle of the remotes ignites the night,
With bickering debates over what's wrong or right,
But the moral of the story, as we jive,
Is we share these moments, oh how we thrive!

Together we stand in this bonkers affair,
With sticky notes and giggles, without any care,
In our quirky abode, every day feels new,
In unity above, there's always a view.

Hearth of Shared Moments

Gather 'round the fireplace, warmth wraps tight,
With marshmallows and laughter, oh what a sight,
We poke at the flames, as stories ignite,
In the hearth of shared moments, all is just right.

The board game nights bring out our wild side,
With strategy battles where pride takes a ride,
Our dice rolls and laughter, louder and louder,
Forget the winner—let's cheer and feel prouder!

Pajama day stretches into silly schemes,
Where bad hair and pillows fuel our dreams,
In our lazy cocoon, let the world pass by,
With giggles and snacks, it's always high time.

So here in our bubble, we plot and we play,
In the hearth of shared moments, we find our way,
Through mischief and fun, we've built up our lore,
Together we dance, who could ask for more?

Heartbeats in Harmony

In the rhythm of chaos, we find our song,
With mischief and mayhem, we all belong,
Every heart beat echoes a silly refrain,
With jokes wrapped in giggles like sunshine after rain.

We dance through the kitchen, all twirls and spins,
With pots as our drums, let the fun begin,
In the melody of spice, and dishes in flight,
Harmony should rule, but we eat what's in sight.

Our plants thrive like weeds—most days with flair,
Their leaves wear our laughter, they don't really care,
While the fridge holds secrets we dare not reveal,
In this raucous place, it's the warmth that we feel.

So here's to our heartbeats, in sync as we twine,
In a dance of our quirks, sparkled with wine,
Through fun and through chaos, let friendship harmonize,

In this jolly old symphony, our spirits will rise!

Embracement in Every Nook

In corners where dust bunnies play,
We gather for tea each quirky day.
The cat wears a hat, quite proud and neat,
While we swap our tales over leftovers to eat.

The couch is a throne for the remote king,
Each button pressed reigns over silly bling.
With laughter that echoes like birds in flight,
We dance in our socks, what a delightful sight!

The fridge hums a tune of forgotten snacks,
Join us in humor, no need for hacks.
We'll tickle the pickle in fun-filled jest,
In our snug little haven, we find all the best!

A slip on the rug leads to giggles galore,
Who knew the mundane could hold so much more?
With every new mishap and each joyful cheer,
Here's to embracing both laughter and cheer!

Sweet Simplicity

A kitchen full of flour, a pancake fight,
Eggs hit the ceiling, oh what a sight!
With laughter our breakfast comes out a mess,
But who needs perfection? We wouldn't want less!

The Java's so strong, it could wake a dead frog,
We sip like we're sipping from a big ol' hog.
Each splash of cream tells a tale so divine,
As we brew up our laughter, cup after line.

With socks that don't match but fit like a dream,
Our fashion's unique, an unmatched team.
We stumble through life, a comedic ballet,
Each day's an adventure; come laugh the day away!

As bedtime approaches, we giggle and yawn,
With monsters in closets all ready to fawn.
Each pillow a friend, each blanket a hug,
In our sweet little chaos, love's the best drug!

The Ties That Shelter

In the yard there's a swing, it's squeaky but bright,
We'll swing into laughter until it's twilight.
With garden gnomes watching our silly charades,
We'll have tea with the flowers, no need for parades.

The laundry's a game where we toss all the socks,
Each finding a match as we laugh at the knocks.
The dogs run in circles, joining our show,
As we tie up our hearts in a joyful tableau.

When rain clouds gather, we're safe from the gloom,
Board games and hot cocoa fill every room.
We'll share our wild dreams, with snacks on our laps,
Each moment a treasure, no time for mishaps!

Fuzzy slippers shuffle, it's a silly parade,
We dance when the sun shines, or even when it's jade.
With each funny story in our cozy retain,
We're tied in our shelter, through joy and through rain!

Harmonious Haven

Welcome to chaos, our sweet little space,
Where socks get misplaced at a frantic pace.
The doorbell's a tune that more often annoys,
But it welcomes our friends, those rascally joys!

Our living room floor becomes a grand stage,
Impromptu performances that spark and engage.
With costumes from closet and props from the shelf,
We become actors while forgetting ourselves!

The garden's a jungle, with weeds we embrace,
Each plant has a story, and each one a face.
With aprons adorned with flour and pride,
We whip up delights that our friends can't abide!

At sunset we gather, all tired and dazed,
Recapping the antics, and how we were praised.
In this joyful cacophony, our hearts intertwine,
In our harmonious haven, everything's fine!

Foundations of Our Dreams

We laid the bricks, one by one,
With laughter loud, we had such fun.
A wobbly wall, a crooked beam,
Yet somehow still, we built a dream.

With goofy plans and mismatched socks,
Our case of nails was full of knocks.
The floorboards creak, a squeaky tune,
Our silly dance beneath the moon.

We painted walls, with colors bright,
Each splash a giggle, pure delight.
A home that sways in silly style,
We'll never tire from this sweet trial.

So here we stand, amid our mess,
With every quirk, we just confess.
The dreams we've built, a grand parade,
In this wild place, our joy displayed.

Walls of Shared Stories

Our walls are scribbled, full of tales,
With mismatched frames, where laughter prevails.
Each photo's a gem, with smiles so wide,
In our quirky gallery, love won't hide.

Our wallpaper's peeling, fondly so,
Reminds us of stunts from long ago.
The kitchen's a stage for culinary art,
With burnt toast memories, we won't depart.

Every crack tells a secret giggle,
In corners where we used to wiggle.
With tales of mishaps on every shelf,
We laugh so hard, we forget ourselves.

From tiny whispers to loud refrain,
Our shared stories bring delightful pain.
In this crazy patchwork of hearts and dreams,
We stitch together what laughter beams.

Embracing Echoes

In our little space, echoes bounce,
Of jokes and quirks that always flounce.
The laughter lingers, spills from the rooms,
Where silly antics brighten the glooms.

Our echoes giggle in every nook,
While each prank hides in a storybook.
With whispered secrets and playful shouts,
We find the joy that true fun's about.

The hallway sways with echoes loud,
As we dance around, like a bustling crowd.
With every step and stomping feet,
We chase our shadows down the street.

So let the echoes ring and play,
In our jolly home, they freely sway.
Together we find, in every sound,
A cozy laughter that knows no bound.

Blueprints of Belonging

With crayons bright, our plans take flight,
Doodles and dreams, a comical sight.
The blueprint laughs, it bends and sways,
As we draw our joy in whimsical ways.

Our plans are silly, our visions whirled,
With towers of snacks and flags unfurled.
Each corner's marked with sticky notes,
Of silly jokes and goat-shaped boats.

Together we scribble, erased some lines,
In this messy world where laughter shines.
With every sketch, a giggle grows,
As friendships flourish like garden rows.

So let's build wide, with hearts as beams,
In our mixture of silliness, life redeems.
Here's to the fun, the love, the cheer,
In blueprints drawn, we find our sphere.

Echoes of Togetherness

In the living room, the cat takes a leap,
The dog thinks it's time for a snack to keep.
We share our laughter, oh what a sight,
Two left feet dancing, a comical plight.

Pajamas are fashion, and socks never match,
We argue who's cooking, with a playful scratch.
Emails unread, but our jokes are on cue,
Echoes of joy, oh how we grew.

A movie night leads to popcorn warfare,
Flying kernels land everywhere without a care.
We laugh at the chaos, the mess we all bring,
Together we find joy in the simple things.

The world outside may be solemn and gray,
But here in our bubble, we get lost in play.
Echoes of giggles dance through the air,
Creating a space that we love to share.

Pillars of Compassion

The fridge is a beast, it grumbles and moans,
We all gather round for its mysterious tones.
Whose turn is it to take out the trash?
A symphony of sighs, and then we all bash.

Hot tea in hand, we spill our hearts wide,
With stories of chaos that make us collide.
Compassion is found in the quirkiest ways,
Like dressing in costumes on lazy, fun days.

We flip through old photos with laughter and glee,
Capturing moments, like the cat in a tree.
Each mishap a chapter, each giggle a song,
In the tapestry woven, we all feel we belong.

Pillars of warmth rise high with each tale,
A fortress of friendship where no one can fail.
Through ups and downs, our bond will stick,
In this joyful chaos, we find the perfect trick.

Stories Drawn in Paint

In the hallway, there's a canvas so grand,
Children's art pieces, a colorful band.
Crayon monsters with three eyes and eight legs,
A masterpiece formed of glitter and pegs.

We swirl in the kitchen, pancakes take flight,
Toppings as wild as our dreams every night.
"More syrup!" we shout, as the laughter runs hot,
Sticky and sweet, a highly prized lot.

The sofa's a ship, sailing pillows of fluff,
Adventure awaits, no journey is tough.
As pirates we battle with giggles and squeals,
Imaginary treasure, oh, how it reveals.

Every corner's a story, a tale to unfold,
In splashes of color, our life is retold.
With brushes of joy, and laughter our paint,
Together we create, our palette, we'll taint.

Whispers of Warmth

Under the blankets, we hide from the chill,
Like cozy coconuts, we settle until.
A whisper with giggles, a secret or two,
Hot cocoa cheers us; it's the best brew.

Our living room turns into a theater grand,
With sock puppets launched by an unseen hand.
We act out the stories, sometimes with flair,
And tumble together in our playful air.

The world can be serious, but here we create,
Moments so silly, we can hardly wait.
With soft, tender whispers that float in the night,
Our hearts are a warm hug that feels oh so right.

Firelight flickers, telling tales of our past,
A beautiful blend of silly and vast.
In this patchwork of love, we forever beam,
Whispers of warmth weave the fabric of our dream.

Bonds Beneath the Ceiling

In the kitchen, flour flies,
The cat does flips, oh my, oh my!
Spaghetti sticks to the ceiling,
While all around, the laughter's reeling.

Socks mismatched on the floor,
Who knew we had a sock store?
Each one's a treasure, so unique,
A quirky way to hear us speak.

We dance in chaos, lose our shoes,
Finding joy in silly blues.
Underneath this roof of dreams,
Life, it bursts at the seams!

From whispers soft to joyful screams,
Shared memories make the best of teams.
With every mishap and grand delight,
Here's where we shine, oh what a sight!

Strength in the Structure

This wall's a bit lopsided, folks,
But it holds up our best silly jokes.
We anchor dreams with paint and nails,
And tell the stories, in epic tales.

The roof has a few leaks to mend,
But does it moan? It learns to bend.
Windows throw a party of light,
As we flip our pancakes just right.

In each corner, laughter rings,
Even when the vacuum sings.
With every creak, there's room for play,
In this odd-place we love to stay.

Tunnels of socks and paper stacks,
We embrace it all without the cracks.
Together we're a comical crew,
Finding strength in the wild and new!

Love's Blueprint

Drawn in crayons, bright and bold,
Plans for laughter never grow old.
Sticky notes around like beams,
Reminders of our wild dreams.

Every room filled with our glow,
From the hallway to the patio.
Blueprints scattered, a big ol' mess,
Yet somehow it all feels like success.

With popcorn ceilings, trippy and fun,
Disco balls when work's all done.
Love's the glue, oh the best kind,
Sticking bits of joy intertwined.

So here's to every quirk and bend,
In this home, our hearts suspend.
With a wink and a pinch of glee,
We design our sweet symphony.

Heartstrings and Timber

Wooden beams holding up our tunes,
While chandeliers dance like cartoon raccoons.
Heartstrings strummed on a wobbly chair,
Echo laughter through the air.

Timber creaks with every cheer,
A symphony we love to hear.
The floors shake with our silly prance,
As we wrap ourselves in a goofy dance.

Nooks filled with pillows, bright and bold,
Each a story waiting to unfold.
Curations of moments, a glorious spree,
In the quirkiest nook, we're truly free.

From the attic down to the hall,
Here's where we answer friendship's call.
In every corner, our joy does shine,
This space is ours, an endless line!

Journeys Under One Sky

We travel in mismatched shoes,
Chasing our hopes like silly fools.
With a map that has no roads,
Laughing at life's crazy codes.

We dance in puddles, splash and play,
Stealing the clouds from the light of day.
With every turn, a joyful jest,
We're lost and found, where we are best.

Each trip a giggle, a tumble down,
Like kids we laugh, we wear the crown.
In every detour, the punchline's bright,
Under one sky, we own the night.

Living Within Love's Embrace

In the kitchen, chaos reigns,
Mixing love with silly stains.
Spaghetti flops, great sauce splatters,
Laughter rings, who cares what matters?

Dancing through rooms with goofy flair,
Wearing socks that do not match, beware!
Every hug a wrestling match,
In our cozy, crazy patch.

We bundle up in mismatched quilts,
Snuggle close, all laughter builds.
With every snort, a happy shout,
Love's silly cuddle is what it's about.

Coalescence of Dreams

In a room where odd things blend,
Bouncing thoughts like kids we send.
Juggling dreams and ice cream too,
Improbable thoughts, we break right through.

We sketch our futures with crayons bold,
Each wild idea, a story told.
In every corner, laughter glows,
Our dreams unite, anything goes.

With pillows piled like silken clouds,
We dive into the laughter loud.
Creating magic in our own way,
Together for a fun-filled stay.

Nest of our Souls

In a nest made with bits and odds,
We gather love, ignore the gods.
Home's not neat, but eyes all shine,
Messy moments are all divine.

We build our dreams with twigs and twine,
Each laugh we share becomes a sign.
Heartstrings tangled in joyful loops,
We're all just silly little troops.

With cookies burned and tea gone cold,
Every mishap is pure gold.
In this nest, no chill exists,
Just warmth, adventure, and silly twists.

Footsteps on Common Ground

We dance and trip on shared old floors,
Each creak a laugh, behind closed doors.
Our socks in colors, of all the hues,
Sliding like experts, we can't win or lose.

Cookies crumble, crumbs in the cracks,
Every snack fight, we make our attacks.
With pillows as shields, we have our fun,
Giggles and laughter 'til the day is done.

Whiskers and tails weave tales in the room,
Chasing their shadows, making hearts bloom.
And if the vase tips over, what a scene!
We'll blame the cat, he was never too keen.

When dishes are piled like mountains so steep,
We sing like it's Broadway, not counting the heap.
Together we shine, a circus so bright,
In this lively chaos, everything feels right.

Pathways of Harmony

We stroll on pathways of mismatched shoes,
In the park where laughter is the main news.
With ice cream drips down our sunny shirts,
Every drop a giggle, the best kind of flirts.

Bubbles float up, a floating parade,
Pop them with joy, is this what we made?
Skipping the puddles, we leap and we bound,
Chasing our dreams, we're lost but we're found.

A picnic spread with sandwiches thick,
Each bite with a story that's sure to stick.
We toast with our juices, a cheer for the day,
To friendship and laughter, hip-hip-hooray!

As the sun sets, we carve tales in the dusk,
Each laugh a sparkle, each moment a musk.
In this sweet journey, through thick and through thin,
Hand in hand always, together we win.

Lanterns in the Night

Under the stars, we light little beams,
Illuminating laughter, painting our dreams.
With marshmallows roasting, the fire pops bright,
Stories swirl upwards into the night.

Mismatched lanterns dance, flicker and sway,
Leading us onward, guiding our play.
With glow sticks in hand, it's a wild parade,
We're glowing with joy; that's how fun is made.

A maze of blankets, forts built with flair,
Every crevice a secret, a moment to share.
With shadows that giggle and whispers that creep,
Adventures unfold as the wishes run deep.

At midnight we'll dream, under thickets of light,
With our heads filled with wonder, we embrace the night.

Through lanterns and laughter, let's spark and ignite,
In the warmth of togetherness, everything's right.

Gardens of Growth

In our garden of joy, we plant seeds of fun,
Watered with giggles, growing one by one.
We dance with daisies, twirl with the breeze,
While the bumblebees buzz, we're happy as peas.

Our veggies do yoga, stretching for sun,
Tomatoes play tag; oh, aren't we the ones?
With carrots like swords, we hold our ground,
Every patch is a playground where laughter is found.

We gather our harvest, a bounty of cheer,
Each pickle we jar brings friends drawing near.
With pies made of dreams, we bake and we play,
In this garden of love, every moment's a ray.

So here's to the blooms, with petals and glee,
In the sunshine of friendship, forever we'll be.
Planting our laughter, nurturing light,
In this garden of growth, everything feels right.

Whispered Wishes

In the kitchen, a spoon's a wand,
Making soup that's less respond.
Noodles float like fish at bay,
Who knew dinner could play this way?

Laughter spills with every pour,
As we try to close the door.
It swings back, with a creak and squeak,
Who knew charades could be this meek?

Our cat steals the spotlight, it's true,
Paws on the table, a culinary coup.
Master Chef in furry disguise,
With whiskers and mischief in its eyes.

So here's a toast to soup and fun,
And to escaping when dishes are done!
Let's make a mess with silly tricks,
Who knew chaos could be so quick?

Tides of Togetherness

In our backyard, a pool of dreams,
Inflatable flamingos, bursting at seams.
Jump in, splash out, what a grand scheme,
But watch out for dives that make you scream!

Picnic blankets fly like kites,
Sandwiches end up in tree heights.
I found a pickle, you found a shoe,
What other treasures wait for our crew?

Sprinklers dance like they know the score,
Water fights break out, and laughter soars.
We chase each other, squeals abound,
And leave our worries lost, not found.

The sun sets low, colors awash,
We gather close for marshmallow posh.
With giggles and stories, we share the beat,
In these waves of joy, life feels complete.

Threads of Our Journey

With mismatched socks, we start our day,
Hopping in grooves only we sway.
Walls echo tunes, we laugh and spin,
Fashion statements, where to begin?

"Your shirt's inside out," I shout with glee,
"Just a new trend," you wink back at me.
Coffee spills like a modern art piece,
As we brew plans that never cease.

Every corner holds a small surprise,
Like missing keys or some rubber flies.
Let's build a fort with pillows galore,
And watch the world through our cardboard door.

In our tapestry, threads intertwine,
Fumbling through moments, like fish in brine.
We'll stitch the days with laughter and cheer,
In every fiber, friendship is clear.

Open Doors and Open Hearts

With squeaky hinges, our doors invite,
Neighbors peeking in, what a sight!
Baking cookies, who'll eat the dough?
Will it be us? The answer is no!

Our living room's a circus ring,
Where cats perform and kids all sing.
Balloons float high, just out of reach,
While we plot our next silly speech.

In the garden, we plant with glee,
Tomatoes sneaking, come have a spree!
We swap our plants, a leafy trade,
With herbal scents, our smells parade.

So if you wander, come take a look,
We share more fun than an open book.
With hearts wide open, bring your cheer,
In this joyful home, you're always near!

www.ingramcontent.com/pod-product-compliance
Lightning Source LLC
Chambersburg PA
CBHW050307120526
44590CB00016B/2527